To those of you most important to me… thank you.

One World, One Tribe

Join the Revolution

The Solution

1. Marijuana
2. Hard Drugs
3. Prostitution

Section 3: Religion

The Problem

1. Empty promise/Empty Threat
2. Removes Responsibility
3. Creates Divisions
4. Recruitment and Retention the Pursuit of Power
5. Drains Resources

The Solution

1. Spirituality Should Be Free

Section 4: One World One Tribe

Intro

Frustrated and angry, I cannot keep my mouth shut any longer. Humanity is capable of so much more and yet we continue to settle for the world as it is now. We currently suffer from a devastated economy, from which we are fully capable of recovery, not recovery eventually but recovery right now. We continue to empower criminals when we are fully capable of removing their ability to profit which is the very source of their power. We continue to allow our social evolution to lag our achievements by holding on to ancient and outdated belief systems, beliefs which create divisions among us and keep us from uniting as a species. We are in a desperate time. The future of our world, as it always has for every generation throughout history, depends on our actions now. In order to make better decisions we must first change some of our thought processes. It will not be easy but it can be done.

Take any great time in our history and you will see there were moments when the greatest of nations/cultures reached a crossroad. It was the decisions they made and actions they took at these crossroads that dictated the future success or failure of their nation. We are at such a crossroad now but it is not a single nation that is at stake, every nation is involved. Our world has shrunk to the point where decisions in one country can affect the entire world. We are truly global and must take it into consideration when we make our decisions and take our actions. Considering other nations, cultures, and ethnic groups is new to our way of thinking. It will not be easy to change the way we think because protecting our own has always been a part of humanity, but it must be done. This world is not mine, yours or theirs it belongs to all of us and we must share in the responsibility for it and each other.

When you read this book please open your mind enough to see the good that can be achieved. Do not focus on one area you in which you disagree. Take the work as a whole. There are certain solutions I will offer where I do not agree with the choices people have made to end up in their situations, but I must set aside my personal beliefs for the greater good. All I can say is their situation exists and will continue to exist so it must be somehow accommodated.

I am not a writer. I am a non-writer who reached a bottom because of no fault of mine. At the bottom I reached a point of clarity. I realized there were three basic problems in our modern world that could be addressed and if they were dealt with properly could have a positive effect on the quality of life for all of us.

I am a victim of the recession. I owned a business I was forced to close because of the collapse in housing. In my business I offered a form of profit sharing a concept I will expand on in section one. In my younger years I experienced the War on Drugs first hand. I saw people

5

tempted by the lure of money and have a firm grasp of how the Illegal Drug Industry empowers criminals. When it comes to religion I studied all faiths extensively before I made my decision to be a humanist. For most, it would be true that I know more about their religion than they do. I won't ask you to abandon your God. I simply wish for you to evaluate the position religion holds in your life.

It is my intention that this work will in the least, stir up a debate and at best start a non-violent revolution. We cannot afford for these areas of our society to continue with the status quo. In each of the areas I will discuss we are failing miserably and offer solutions. It is my intention that this work be used to start a nonpartisan nonprofit organization dedicated to implementing the solutions offered here. Our world is in a bad place and I for one can't take it anymore. Join the Revolution, One World One Tribe.

Economy

Problem

If you do not understand why we are in a recession the answer is actually quite simple. The banking industry was not regulated in the area of home loans and therefore made it extremely easy for unqualified applicants to access loans they could not afford. Why did this cause a problem? It created a false economic boom by creating a false demand for homes which could never be sustained. While it created hundreds of thousands of real estate related jobs, wages outside of the real estate industry were not keeping up with the rise in the price of homes. When reality caught up to the fairytale our economy collapsed. We also face a challenge in the proper way to deal with the wealthy. Are the wealthy a problem? Yes they are, and are in need of being dealt with because they have been allowed to gain too much control. It is widely known that capitalism continues to widen the margin of separation between the middle class and the wealthy. It is the control held by the wealthy that allowed for the real estate problems in the first place. Now I want to make sure you understand that I do not wish to eliminate the wealthy or the ability to become wealthy. I merely believe the wealthy have obtained an unfair advantage and need to be put in check. I will propose radical changes to the way capitalism is allowed to operate without removing the ability to obtain wealth. We can solve the problems which currently exist in our economy and create a sustainable economy, but most importantly we can do this right now.

NO DOC LOANS: "No Doc Loans" were at the core of the problem. The regulators allowed for a type of loan qualification which was originally created to assist small business owners to obtain a home loan. "No Doc" means no documentation of income was necessary to qualify. The two things an applicant was required to have to qualify were a proper down payment and a statement of income. People were actually allowed to say what their income was without having to prove it. Banks felt it was a safe loan to make because the business owners were believed to be financially educated and experienced enough to self regulate. The banks also believed people would not falsify any statement of income nor obtain a loan which they could not afford. With a substantial enough down payment loan officers also felt a false sense of security that the banks could recover their money if the homeowner did actually default. No one at the banks realized the potential disaster they were creating. Loan officers soon found a way to qualify anyone with a large enough down payment for the maximum their down payment could afford. I do not know what amount the down payment needed to be of the actual loan. All I know is several people took out loans of greater amounts than they could afford business owners as well as non-business owners.

I got my license to build in 2004 which was towards the end of the boom. Being a new Contractor no one would touch me for building a new home from the ground up so I started on the floor, literally. I knew I had to prove myself before I could gain the more lucrative contracts. While I developed my flooring business I ended up being offered a partnership to open a flooring retail business. It seemed like a great idea at the time to be able to make money off the material as well as the installation. Without much money we were able to finagle a lease space and the wholesale vendors were more than eager to supply us with the necessary showroom displays. They even gave us enough products to do the entire floor of the showroom in order to display the installed product. We were open in 30 days. I sold out to my partner within ten months and they closed within a total of fourteen months. During the time when we were giving it our best to build a business we were doing light kitchen and bath remodels. One thing I liked to do when we went out to a new neighborhood was pick up the flyers of houses for sale close to where we were working. I never failed to be amazed at the price people were asking for their homes. I can remember saying "What the heck are these people doing for a living to be able to afford these prices?" At the time I did not notice the increase in the number of homes for sale. It was a sign of what was about to happen. I also was not privy to the information about the no doc loan which was how many of these homes were sold in the first place. The increase in the number of homes for sale was the result of people who were falling behind in payments and trying to salvage their equity by selling their home. Not a bad plan but there was a major problem. There were too many people about to be in the same predicament. It seemed like overnight the market was flooded with homes and yet people were still not recognizing there was a problem. The banks were slow to react. As the housing market continued to saturate I was on vacation with my family at the end of June, 2008. I noticed the stock market was showing signs that the days of the easy money was coming to an end. I thought, much like most people, it was merely a periodic downturn. And just like many others I did not realize the real estate boom was over.

I returned from my vacation to complete the remodel job I had going at the time. It was an impossible idea to think it would be my last remodel. After it ended I spent a little money trying to drum up some more business. The ad budget was spent in vain. Through a home designer contact of mine I was able to manage a few leads. Two of the leads were for home additions and one was for commercial office shell for an attorney which was perfectly located behind one of the courthouses downtown. I was happy for a moment. The moment would not last long. First the designer called and said the homeowners were having issues getting their home equity loan. As usual I offered up my loan officer contacts thinking they may be able to help.

Then the moment of truth came in a phone call from the attorney. He told me the bank said there was a freeze on all commercial lending. His office building would not come to be. Within moments of the phone call I was dialing up my loan officer friend. He not only confirmed the freeze on commercial lending but said there was a freeze on all loans unless they were of the highest credit rating and income was above the standard required amounts. He said he did not know "what the hell was going on."

Wrap your mind around this; do you realize how many industries were/are supported by the real estate industry? Now I hope I don't leave any out.

<u>DIRECT</u>: Manufacturers, Wholesale and Retail

Building Material	Furniture	Utilities
Banking	Real Estate Agents	Paving
Equipment (small)	Equipment (large)	Designers
Appliance	Electronics	Linens
Window Covering	Landscaping	Maid
Pest Control	Shipping	Transportation
Mechanic	Fuel	Marketing

INDIRECT: EVERYTHING ELSE! People in the industries listed above spend money on everything and without them EVERYTHING is affected.

Think about it. Hundreds of thousands of people were first put into unemployment and then into underemployment, including myself. I make a fraction of what I used to while I was a builder/remodeler and I was a Cost Plus builder which means I sold my services at a discount to regular contractors. So for me to take a pay cut is nowhere near as close to the pay cuts that many others out there have been forced to take. How many of you reading this now know someone or is someone that fits this description? Answer, too many of us!

Part of the reason there was so much money available for the loan industry to distribute to unqualified borrowers was because of the enormous amount of funds accumulated by the wealthy class. It was demand for investments by the wealthy that created the complex loan funding schemes. Now investing their money can never be viewed as a bad thing to do because everyone should invest when they have available funds. The only problem with the investment was there were not enough legitimate borrowers. You already know the result from what you read above. If the wealthy were at the root of the problem what made it so?

THE WEALTHY: To be a wealthy person is not in its own right a detriment to society, nor is the accumulation of wealth. It is only when the wealthy abuse free market unrestricted capitalism to obtain an unfair advantage over the working and middle classes. It seems as if the wealthy were to have their way they would subjugate the masses to do their bidding. Of course not all wealthy people think this way.

I was a child of the Reagan "trickle down" era and actually believed in the concept. I later realized it does not work. Wealthy people simply accumulate wealth. It is not in their nature to share. For those of you who are thinking of the philanthropic activities by the wealthy you must understand such actions are motivated more by ego than charity. To understand how a truly unregulated free market operates it is as simple as the game "Monopoly." In the game people begin to collect property from which they can collect rents when another player lands on them. Every time a player passes "Go," they receive an income but the income does not keep up with the inflation as other players increase their rent revenues by improving their properties. Eventually there becomes an advantage by some players with more improved properties than the others. They begin to eliminate the others when the players land on their properties and cannot afford to pay the rents, even after they mortgage all their properties (a good example of a credit driven economy). Without incomes following the inflation of the rents combined with the limited amount of credit available eventually the game ends with one player bankrupting the rest. Now it might seem like an over simplification but the reality is the basic fundamentals of the game are mirrored in the real world economies.

I do not know where the statistic originated but I hear it over and over again that in the United States the top one percent control over ninety seven percent of the wealth. Now if the country has a population of approximately three hundred million people that would mean two hundred and ninety one million people are forced to live off of three percent of the country's wealth. To me three percent shared by the majority seems an unfair distribution. Let me say it again, I am not against the acquisition of wealth. I just feel like the wealthy individuals and corporations are building their wealth on the backs of their employees rather than in partnership with them. We are a technological society still using the industrial business model. It is time for it to evolve. I will revisit the concept of partnering with employees later in this work.

During a conversation, through a series of internet postings, with a friend of mine he spoke of taxing the wealthy at a higher percent than others as punishing them for their success. He also spoke of the need for a flat tax. I could relate to his argument because I once thought the same way. But then again I used to be a republican and have an imaginary friend named God. Both of which I am proud to say I have evolved away from.

I tried to explain that if a person is making more they should pay more but he did not understand. I will try to clear it up here. If you take 100 marbles and divide them into two piles. The first pile has 97 marbles. And the second has 3 marbles. If we are not to expect the pile with 97 marbles to contribute at a larger percentage then we are in effect asking the pile of 3 marbles to cover the larger portion of our government. If we chose to have the government operate off a budget of 3 marbles then what is it that we should sacrifice first? Pick from the following list:

DEA	FBI	NAVY
Air Force	ARMY	Marines
Interstate Highway	FDA	SEC
Police	Fire Dept.	Etc.

The list above are but a few things I could think of off the top of my head. Just think about what the Federal, State and Local Governments provide for us to make us a First World Country. Yes, we could lower, eliminate or choose a flat tax, but it would weaken us and turn us in the direction of a Third World Country if we ever allow it.

Look into history and study the causes of many of the revolutions. You will find the wealthy of the country had reached the point where their collection of wealth was detrimental to the society. After a while the concept of each individual having equal opportunity to obtain wealth becomes laughable as incomes continue to be lowered and inflation continues to rise. The situation reaches that of the Middle Ages with landlord and serf. There is no economic growth and other than the wealthy everyone else suffers through a subsistence type of living. How many people reading this are living paycheck to paycheck right now or close to it? Our current state of affairs would show that we are heading directly towards a modern version of serf and landlord.

Large Corporations are taking steps to break the back of labor in America. The steps they are taking will lower wages and benefits for American workers.

1. Outsourcing jobs overseas.
    a. Employees will cause less problems with the threat of their job disappearing. The incomes in the U.S. are already lower as a result.
2. Debt
    a. Both consumer and educational debt has risen because of the lower wages people are forced to borrow in order to afford

anything. An employee in debt will not cause any problems because they will fear losing their job.

3. Health
   a. Without universal or affordable healthcare people live with the insecurity of illness ruining them financially.

Corporations are using the three factors above to regain control over labor. They lost the control when the unions gained strength in the early 1900's. Many middle class and blue collar people today do not know the history of the period. Without the actions the unions took then we would not have a middle class today.

Do you want to live in a world where wages are forced so low that you must have more than one job to afford to survive? Where retirement becomes a myth? Vacations disappear and healthcare is for the wealthy?

The Solution

In economics there is a term called "Demand" which to put it simply means the amount of buyers there are for products and services. What creates demand? It is simple, Income creates demand. It is income that allows people to afford products and services. The greater the number of people with incomes large enough to purchase an item the greater the demand will be. In recent years I have heard a lot about supply side economics. Supply side economics from what I can understand means products and services are produced at lower costs making them more affordable to lower income earners. To my simple mind supply side economics is faulty. A product can be sold for a penny but if I do not have the penny to purchase it there is no demand for the product from me. We are in a state where there is nearly no demand for housing because there are not enough people who can afford the homes even when they are at a thirty percent discount or greater. The supply is there and the price is low but there are no incomes to create the demand. I am sure that many of you out there reading this can relate to the idea of things being out of reach financially at the moment.

It just so happens that I am writing this the day after Labor Day 2010. I spent one of the days with my family strolling around the Old Town area of my city. I noticed that several of the shops had signs in the windows of "50% OFF Everything in the store." In one of the more artsy, gallery type stores I started a conversation with the owner. I asked about how they were handling the economy and if it was affecting their business. She proceeded to tell me there were twenty businesses that closed in Old Town since January. She also shared with me a statistic stating conventions were down sixty percent for 2010. I was told conventions are the major demand for their products because it is conventions that bring out of state visitors. Even at fifty percent of the stores were not ringing sales. The gallery I visited prior to the shop owned by the lady with all of the interesting, but depressing, stats the artist there had opened a conversation with me asking where we were from. He was upbeat and friendly but there was a definite disappointment which he tried to hide when he found out we were locals. He obviously knew we were not his target customer, we were not tourists. He proceeded to tell me "it must be local's day" because all the people he had spoken with were locals. I jokingly asked if he thought it was the economy and that maybe the reason for the local traffic was because people could not afford to travel for the holiday weekend. After the discussion with the lady at the neighboring gallery I wish I would never had mentioned anything to him about the economy. I felt like I had poured salt on a wound. He was already too well aware of the situation with the economy.

I purposely leave out the name of my city because it is irrelevant. These types of stories are happening everywhere.

The solutions I am about to offer come from a combination of my educational studies and my experience both as an employee and a small business owner. If you do not agree with these ideas then I challenge you to come up with better ones.

GIVE THE WORLD A RAISE: I will repeat something I said earlier to emphasize the point "Income creates demand." At the time I am writing this, NBC Nightly News just reported it is estimated that 18.9 million people in the United States are unemployed, which equals 9.6%, and that another 8.9 million people are working part time because they cannot find full time employment. One thing I do not support is relying on government intervention in the economy but there have been several points in history where it has been necessary. This is one of those times.

If you do the math, it means approximately 177,975,000 are working in the United States. I believe the necessary boost to the economy can be created for a mere $1.00 per hour. Let me explain, to keep the example simple I will use a thirty hour work week to account for the number of part-time workers. My proposal for a short term boost to demand is to give every person working a $1.00 per hour raise. It does not matter at what level their current income is at, from minimum wage through executives. There is no need for a cutoff point based on income; we would not want to be accused of discriminating against the more affluent citizens. I'm sure once the politicians get a hold of the idea there will be several complex rules and stipulations added to what should be a very basic idea.

In the United States alone the numbers are as follows:

$177,975,000 (new income per hour generated by $1.00 per hour raise x working population)

X 30 hours (hours per work week.)

$5,339,250,000 per week and an amazing $277,641,000,000 annually

Yes, you are reading this correctly; over five billion per week would be pumped back into the hands of people who spend it. More importantly, over two hundred and seventy seven billion pumped into the economy over the course of a year. How is that for creating demand?

In comparison, the President Obama's stimulus package is estimated at 50 billion in total. I'm not trying to knock President Obama, I believe he is doing the best he can with the resources available.

I propose this raise not only be implemented in the United States but in every country with which the United States does trade. We are in a global economy and the world must follow suit.

Would you like to see the numbers for China? Again to keep it simple I will use the same percentages of population working for the example. Which means approximately 590 million Chinese are currently working.

$590,000,000

<u>X 30 hours</u>

$17,700,000,000 per week and $920,400,000,000

I understand in lesser developed nations the wages are lower than in the United States. For the sake of this example it can be computed as a percentage of the Federal Minimum Wage and that percentage used in those countries where wages are lower. The next section "Global Minimum Wage" will address the problems of lower wages from one country to another.

Honestly, I do not believe such a solution could ever successfully be put in place because it requires government intervention in private industry at a level too imposing for any government action. Since this solution will requires government intervention and therefore would never come to be I do offer a solution that does not require any government involvement, see the Profit Sharing section below.

GLOBAL MINIMUM WAGE: Once the economy gets its initial boost there must be policies put in place that allow for the upturn to continue. One concept, Global Minimum Wage, can solve some of the issues.

Now I understand completely that the entire third world cannot immediately come up to the Federal Minimum Wage of the United States without creating an enormous stress of inflation. It would have to be a gradual increase with a deadline in the next three to five years. At the time of the deadline all trading partners should be at the same rate and those who are not in compliance should be dropped from trading with the other countries.

Countries where the wages will dramatically increase will experience a higher standard of living. The lowest people on the pay scale will afford to create demand a whole new demand of their own. Yes, it will come with a bit of inflation but it will not be too large to be absorbed. See the "Note on Inflation" for a detailed explanation.

A NOTE ON INFLATION: In my state the current minimum wage is $7.50 per hour. To raise it by a dollar to $8.50 is a 13.34% increase in labor. Now each industry has a percentage of sales that is used as a standard for labor budgets. For example in the fast food industry the standard is 25%. Twenty percent is non-management labor and five percent is for management. Now using the restaurant industry as my example I will show you how inflation is easily absorbed by the increase in wages, and to emphasize my point I will say that all of the wages will increase by the 13.34% which would be larger than a dollar for those making more than minimum wage. But, for the sake of the example I will show all wages increasing by the same percentage.

Labor Budget (as a % of Sales)	25%
Multiplied by	13.34%
Equals an inflation of	3.4%

Potential Inflation dollar for dollar the labor increase)	3.4%	(absorbs
New Labor budget inflation)	28.4%	(without

Of course this is a simplified example but it is easy to see how the numbers work. Over time the industry will correct itself to the 25% labor budget. Just think for a moment how many times in the past 20 years that the minimum wage has increased. I can remember when congress called the Presidents and CEO's of McDonalds and Pizza Hut to testify before congress on how their industries would be impacted if the minimum wage was increased. They made some outrageous claims like they would have to reduce the staff, their industry would struggle, and they might possibly be forced to shut some locations down. Both companies are still around and flourishing...well except for the unrelated impact of the current economy.

The Clinton/Gore administration understood the concept of economic demand in relation to income. The example above is from their first term. Many critics of their administration point to the explosion of the internet for the economic boom the United States experienced during their tenure. I will not deny the internet played a large part during those years but the data supports the upturn began shortly after the raise in the minimum wage. In fact the effects of raising the minimum wage can easily be tracked and proved positive in its results through historical data. Raising wages is one way to create demand but like I stated above the industries eventually correct back to their desired budget percentages, which translates to inflation and results in a diminished purchasing power by those who received the raise in the first place. In the next section I will discuss "Profit Sharing." I believe it solves the need for the periodic adjustments to wages.

PROFIT SHARING: This is something very near and dear to my heart because I actually proved it works while operating my construction company. Now in the construction industry I started with hard surface flooring. The original labor budget for hard surface flooring was 50% of sales. We are talking installation sales and not material.

When I first got started I tried to pay people hourly and noticed something that I knew existed but had never experienced firsthand. The installers were making sure they got a full day's work in even if the job did not warrant it. In some cases their actions erased the profitability of the job or caused a loss. I quickly made a change to piece work. Some competitors paid piece work and I knew how much per square foot I needed to pay. But, I did not want the workers to just rush through the projects to increase their pay and possibly jeopardize quality. Plus, there were certain parts to the install process which were not covered in a piece work type agreement. So, I changed it to a percentage payout. I took the total amount of labor related sales and multiplied it by 70%. Sounds obscene right?

Well an interesting thing happened when we started the percentage payout. More people wanted to work for me. The quality of the work went up and so did the production. The industry standard was 200 square feet per day. We were averaging three hundred to three hundred and fifty square feet per day. The employees became engaged in the company. They each had a vested interest in every single bid we made. I could literally sit down with them and we could figure our price based on what they knew they could produce in a day to make the money they wanted to make. Our prices ended up smoking the competition. We could lower our prices because the install teams knew what they were capable of completing in a given time frame. And the part I like best is the overhead and profit were covered in every project, no budget overruns. Calculating out insurance and overhead, I made a solid 20% profit on every single project.

Practically overnight our business increased. One of my lead guys actually calculated his earnings at $37.50 per hour, for installing tile! In our market a comparable position would receive a maximum of $16.00 per hour as a lead installer. Several competitors actually tried stealing some of my crews and they just laughed because no one could pay them what I paid them. The competitors simply could not grasp the concept.

I am an avid viewer of the business channel and often hear them speak about tax rates on the wealthy. Without coming out a stating it directly they still promote the same idea as "Trickle Down Economics" of the Reagan/Bush era. Well, I don't think we need to raise the taxes on the wealthy or the large corporations. I believe there is a much more beneficial program to be implemented and it does not require government intervention or policy. At this point I will talk about a different type of demand moving away from the economic definition. I would like to introduce the demand of the people. It is a concept which can be traced back to the very inception of our country with the Declaration of Independence. "We the People..." so the concept is at the core of American Values.

I recommend watching the documentary "Capitalism: A love Story" by Michael Moore. In his documentary he reveals a letter to the top investors of a large corporation, one which was involved with the bailouts, where they actually acknowledge their control over government policy and action. In one part of their letter they acknowledge the only thing that could possibly affect their control is the majority of the population stepping up and challenging them. In other words, they mean a revolution of sorts. Now I don't mean a revolution where the there is violence and certain "aristocratic" types lose their head. No, those types of revolutions have run their course. I also am against unions because of the potential for corruption. The modern version of a revolution is much more peaceful.

What do I mean when I say "demand of the people?" The people do not realize it but they ultimately hold complete power. Let's say the employees of the top five retailers or the top five restaurant chains decided to demand a share of the profits. Without need for unions or union dues the entire workforce could pressure the corporations to agree to their demands. As a small business owner I believe in partnering with my employees whenever it is possible. My example in my construction company was equal to 50% of profits. I think 50% can easily be afforded by the majority of companies. It is after all coming from profits and is not a cost of production. What would happen if the employees of all the major corporations demanded a 50% profit share or they would walk out? I think they would immediately get some serious attention. Do you think the world's largest retailers and restaurant chains could afford to have their entire work force walk out? The power is with the people and it is time for them to take it.

The "fat cat" executives receive millions in bonuses. They are not tied to their employees so it becomes a situation where the employees are a cost that affects their bonuses. This is not the way it should be, because it motivates the management to push the labor costs as far down as possible. It creates a conflict between management and laborers. Eventually, when the labor is pushed down far enough it requires government intervention to be lifted such as in the case of raising the minimum wage. If profit share is to work correctly it must not have any imbalances. From the top executive to the entry level employee the bonuses must be equal; the potential for greed is removed because it creates a united team with a singular goal.

Like I said before, the power is with the people. But, it is not limited to the employees themselves. Consumers can choose to only frequent those businesses that profit share. I envision a world where there will be a sticker on the door of the business, right next to the sticker showing what credit cards are accepted, which will show the company as a profit sharing company. Maybe it will be a gold star for 50% profit share and a silver star for 25% profit share. Then consumers can choose where to spend their dollars.

When developing the idea of profit sharing I ran into several issues to be addressed. Some of the issues were how to deal with seasonal businesses, losses, and proper distribution of profit sharing.

To figure out when to distribute profits most businesses can do so monthly but there are some businesses that are seasonal and profit sharing must not be detrimental to the health of the business. For an example I will use a family owned ice cream shop. In the ice cream business the majority of profits are made in the three month period of summer and much of those profits have to cover the losses incurred during autumn, winter and early spring. In the case of seasonal businesses only an annual distribution of profit sharing would work without creating stress on the finances of the business.

Losses in a business can be accounted for with ease. Whether it is a monthly distribution of profit sharing or profits are distributed annually it is only fair that losses be deducted from future profit share. If losses are not accounted for in the formula of profit sharing then the program could possibly become a detriment to the survivability of the business.

Proper distribution of profit sharing should be an easy formula, and one that can be understood by all employees. It also should be fair to all employees. For example a part time employee should not receive the same dollar amount as a full time employee for obvious reasons. Also, there may be the case where there are multiple locations or multiple units as we call them in the restaurant industry. If one unit's profits are larger than another then the differences must be accounted for in the formula. The employees should always be rewarded in direct relation to their time, commitment and the success of the company or unit operations depending on the structure of the company.

Below is an example of the most simple profit sharing formula:

Employee	Monthly Hours	
Manager	180	45 hours/wk * 4wks
Assistant Manager	180	
Full Time Emp.	160	40 hours/wk * 4wks
Full Time Emp.	160	
Part Time Emp.	100	25 hours/wk * 4wks
Part Time Emp.	100	
Total Hours	880	

Profit for the Month $10,000

Formula: (Profit/2)/Total Hours=Profit Share per Hour

$10,000/2 = $5,000

$5,000/880 = $5.68 Profit Share per Hour

Employee Profit Share for the month: Profit Share per Hour* Hours Worked

Employee	Monthly Hours		$Share/mo
Manager	180	* $5.68 =	$1022.40
Assistant Manager	180	* $5.68 =	$1022.40
Full Time Emp.	160	* $5.68 =	$908.80
Full Time Emp.	160	* $5.68 =	$908.80
Part Time Emp.	100	* $5.68 =	$568
Part Time Emp.	100	* $5.55 =	$568
			$4998.40

Of course the example is simplified. The numbers will obviously vary from business to business and also by industry. But, no matter what size the profit sharing payment is to the employees it provides a new opportunity between employee and employer. It creates a type of partnership between them. An employee sharing in the profits also should now have a vested interest in the success of the company rather than feeling like they are merely working to make the owner rich.

Some other areas of concern when implementing a profit sharing program are normal wages, benefits and raises.

Wages, it should be understood, will be at the market rate based on the position. A minimum wage position will still be a minimum wage position and a manager will still be a manager and each employee should expect to be paid market rate accordingly. When hiring new employees the companies should not feel obligated to share profit sharing information with prospects and only share information once the new hire has completed all necessary training. Training period should be agreed upon by the employees to eliminate any corruption of the process by management.

Along with 50% of profits there should be 50% representation on all board of directors. The democratic system should be implemented for all company policy.

Benefits differ in each organization and should be addressed by the company as a team. Benefits may be something the company could vote on because of the new understanding by, and information shared with the employees they will get to see how each benefit impacts the profitability of the company.

Raises could be handled much in the same way. When the needs of the company are discussed with the employees they will better understand the challenges they face and be able to offer their input. A situation where wages and raises could become an issue is when a company has a skilled position and the market rate for the position has increased. Let's say for the sake of the example that the employee in the position has brought it to the attention of management that they were offered more money to join a different company. The employees could choose to meet on the issue, discuss the options and put it to a vote. The employees may feel the current employee is worth keeping and agree to a raise or they might find a different solution altogether. Therein lays the hidden power of profit sharing, shared profit equals shared responsibility.

TAXES, A BALANCED BUDGET AND THE DEFICIT: A side note on the potential impact on income tax revenue. If the majority of the people could acquire positions with profit sharing companies then the tax revenue at the federal level would increase. In other words the wealthy could keep their tax breaks since the majority of the population would be earning more money and therefore paying more taxes the federal government would not be so impacted by the revenue from the wealthy or the corporations. The country might actually reach a point where the budget could be balanced and payments made to lower the deficit.

POTENTIAL REVENUE INCREASES: Every time the minimum wage has been raised in the United States a revenue growth for businesses followed. It is not hard to imagine just how much revenues would increase if the entire work force was now sharing in 50% of the profits. To put it in the most simple of terms, more people could afford more things. Remember, you do not need to fear inflation because profit sharing will balance it out.

One key requirement to profit sharing is 100% transparency. All financial data for the company must be shared without any omissions. Profit Sharing can work and should be demanded by all employees, right now.

COOPERATIVES: While operating my construction company I realized yet another potential for reform. When I looked at the way homes were built with several sub-contractors working for the general contractor I noticed there was a potential to coop the process of building a home. If the real estate industry had not tanked I might have had the time to develop the idea further but we all know what happened. However, I did do some research running mock scenarios and using estimations when good data was unavailable. In my limited research I found the possible effects of cooping the building of a home could lower overhead and in doing so increase the profits of the project or lowering the price of the home. If it could work in building, then would it not work elsewhere?

After a little research on coops I realized there are a few out there and they are holding their own against regular free market competitors. I think coops have proved they work and can do so in any industry if properly implemented.

Some of the same basic fundamentals of profit sharing apply to coops as well, such as wages for each position at market rate and distribution of profits based on time invested. Same formula as above except for the percentage of distribution of profits is 100%. Of course, there would need for the allowance of a certain amount of cash to remain in the coop for operations and growth. All of the details would be worked out by the coop members as they chose.

I think cooperatives should be formed in every industry to compete against for profit companies.

Drugs, Crime and Prostitution

The Problem

The problem in dealing with drugs and crime is many times certain actions are deemed criminal when there is no real crime committed. If we can allow ourselves to revisit how we define what becomes a criminal act then we could eliminate much of the problems we deal with today. Obvious crimes are property (theft or damage), violence and murder. But, we have criminalized two things that I strongly disagree with, drugs and prostitution. The distribution of a product or service to people who are in demand of the product or service should not be a crime. To criminalize the addict is on offense against basic human nature. To criminalize such acts creates the industries that operate and commit actual crimes to protect their industry which we wage war against. In other words we have actually created our own enemy. Most people reading this will never use the services or choose the profession of a prostitute. The fact remains that prostitution exists in every city, in every state/province and in every country. It is time we revisit, not the morality involved with Drugs and Prostitution, but the laws created to deal with them.

Drugs

The illegal drug industry is a 300 Billion dollar per year global business. (Source "Drug's Inc." NGEO Channel)

HARRY ANSLINGER: Federal Bureau of Narcotics Harry Anslinger quotes taken from Wikipedia.org:

"There are 100,000 total marijuana smokers in the US, and most are Negroes, Hispanics, Filipinos and entertainers. Their Satanic music, jazz and swing, result from marijuana usage. This marijuana causes white women to seek sexual relations with Negroes, entertainers and any others."

"Colored students at the Univ. of Minn. partying with (white) female students, smoking [marijuana] and getting their sympathy with stories of racial persecution. Result: pregnancy"

"Two Negros took a girl fourteen years old and kept her for two days under the influence of hemp. Upon recovery she was found to be suffering from syphilis."

Going against recommendations from the American Medical Association he persuades Congress to outlaw marijuana in 1937. The Drug War begins.

"Since the 1970's the War on Drugs has cost American tax payers over two trillion dollars," from Drugs Inc. by National Geographic Channel. I would ask the reader, would you not rather have spent the money on the deficit?

In the same program it was stated that 41% of Americans have admitted trying Marijuana, including one President.

The quotes and statements above are limited to Marijuana. They were chosen to be included here to show the original issue with narcotics was one of discrimination rather than the drugs themselves. Yes, I do agree there should be some sort of control over narcotics but the current strategy is not only failing to stop usage but is creating many more problems from the criminal organizations producing and distributing the narcotics. The misinformation on narcotics was blown so out of proportion that lawmakers were convinced to the point where they not only outlawed the narcotics but actually criminalized addiction. To criminalize addiction goes against everything good in humanity. So instead of protecting the public from the drug menace the policies enacted created more danger and greater costs which have increased both in the public and private sectors since the war on drugs began.

I have extensive experience and knowledge of how the illegal drug industry operates. I know people who have participated in the industry. Let me make it perfectly clear that I am not a drug user. I am not a "Pot Head" smoker wanting to legalize Marijuana so I can smoke. I do not smoke Marijuana. However, I will admit to having experimented with certain narcotics in my younger years but they did not appeal to me so I simply moved on. My purpose here is much larger than simply making Marijuana available to the smokers; it is about destroying the industry behind narcotics which causes the real crimes of violence, murder, and corruption. To win the War on Drugs is so simple I believe the politicians are bordering on moronic not to realize the solution. To win the War on Drugs you simply need to remove the ability to profit from the production and distribution of the drug. If there is no profit there is no purpose for the industry. Without profit the business of drug cartels (producers), street gangs and independent sellers (distributors) will collapse overnight. The problem is too many people are caught up in fighting the good fight and refuse to accept the fact that the war cannot be won with the current policies. It is up to the people to demand a change in policy. We cannot eliminate the burden of narcotics but we can tremendously lower the costs.

This entire book is based on finances, because I believe the basis of most of our problems lay in the financial realm. I believe the root of most societal problems is financial in one form or another. If you can recall, earlier in this work I did ask you to "*Take the work as a whole. There are certain solutions I will offer where I do not agree with the choices people have made to end up in their situations, but I must set aside my personal beliefs for the greater good. All I can say is their situation exists and will continue to exist so it must be somehow accommodated.*"

Let's discuss the makeup of the industry. The first thing that must be recognized is the demand for the product. It does not matter which narcotic we are speaking of because there is a demand for each of them. One difference is the demand is greater for some than others. Another difference between each narcotic is some actually can create an addict. The two should be dealt with in different ways.

Marijuana

Marijuana is credited with being the narcotic which creates the greatest amount of funding for the organized crime syndicates known as drug cartels. It also has the greatest amount of support from the medical community and continues to be considered a drug that does not need to be illegal. The problem with Marijuana is not with the drug itself but with public perception and the criminal industry behind it. Over my life I have known a number of Marijuana users and it is no different to them than alcohol is to a social drinker. None of the users I know would fall under the definition of an addict. With the exception of some of the studies generated for propaganda, I do not believe Marijuana ever has been nor can be proven addictive. To this day I have not heard any Marijuana user say they are experiencing withdrawals. Not one of them has ever committed a crime because they need their fix from

Marijuana. The smokers I know simply enjoyed an occasional smoke. I have never seen nor heard of an overdose from Marijuana. I do not believe it is medically possible to overdose from Marijuana. In fact a common joke amongst Marijuana smokers is "once you are high, smoking more dope doesn't make you any higher it just makes low on dope." I would go so far as to say that I have seen several more detrimental actions by smokers of nicotine cigarettes as they are having their nicotine fits, and nothing comparable by Marijuana smokers. It is time we end our war against Marijuana.

Hard Drugs

Unlike Marijuana, the harder drugs like heroin, meth, ecstasy and any other drug which a person can verifiably become addicted to or overdose from creates multiple problems and the solutions are not as simple as simply legalizing the drug. Such drugs do share the same criminal enterprise behind them and we have already discussed the crime is not in the production and distribution but in the criminal acts the organizations partake in to protect their business. The users of these drugs become addicted which creates a totally new problem not experienced with Marijuana. The users now need to have their drugs because they are dependent on them. It is not a social form of entertainment, although it may have started out that way, it is a straight addiction. Many times addictions will lead to medical problems. Addictions can also make a person desperate and desperate people will often turn to criminal acts if it means they can get their drugs. Forcing the addicts to live outside the law creates more than just legal issues.

THE INDUSTRY: The problems from the industry are well known. The cartels and street gangs use violence to control their business. We are all well aware of these actual crimes from the news and the glamorization in film. As I write this, Mexico is in a state of turmoil with two competing cartels vying for control of the bordering cities to the United States. Corruption, violence and death run rampant. Such crimes are mirrored on a smaller scale on the United States side of the border. It is well known that street gangs compete for territory in all the major cities. Again, I will say that none of these criminal organizations would have the resources to wage their wars if not for the profit provided by the industry.

THE ADDICT: The addict can become a true criminal. I mean they can actually begin committing real crimes which I have discussed above. Some addicts may partake in the industry and become a producer or a seller. Other addicts will choose to commit theft or burglary where there is a potential for violence. Some will turn to prostitution. In most cases these crimes can be avoided entirely if we chose to treat the addict like we do any other addict and treat them rather than criminalizing their addiction.

HEALTHCARE COSTS: The addict creates medical issues and a costly burden on the health care system. Many of these issues have been recognized in other works and are common knowledge so I will not go into great detail. We already know, infected needles can pass the AIDS virus and other diseases. Overdoses cause strain on the emergency rooms of hospitals, which are often not compensated for the care. A more recent medical cost is related to meth, and can be found in the burn units of hospitals. There you will find addicts, fueled by their addiction, who began producing meth in their makeshift labs to supply their own habit. It was during their production of the drug that they became aware of the highly explosive nature of some of the components used in the production of meth. Their kettles used to cook the meth exploded on them creating flash burns on their body and an uncompensated burden on the hospitals which care for them. In the program Drugs Inc. by the National Geographic Channel, it was estimated the healthcare costs created by meth users alone is $864 million annually in the United States.

Outside of the United States, countries with less resources, battle the drug cartels at a serious disadvantage. Picture a world where the mayor of your city or town must travel with an armed escort. Envision a world where all of your law enforcers must wear masks to hide their identity not only for their safety but for the safety of their families. During America's prohibition era, when the mafias and the bootleggers operated in the same manner of the drug cartels of today, the United States experienced something close to what is happening outside of her borders now. It was obvious that prohibition was an unwinnable war and was repealed. When it comes to narcotics and the Drug War we are in much the same situation. It is time to repeal the laws on Narcotics.

PROSTITUTION: Prostitution is nothing new to human society. It is well documented to have existed throughout our history. The only thing that changes is how each society views prostitution morally and the laws they enact to deal with it. Many people argue the point that it is simply wrong to sell one's body. Others will speak of the potential for human trafficking which they argue is a possible if not common result of the industry of prostitution. The fact remains that just like the laws which created the War on Drugs, the laws against prostitution do not eliminate prostitutes.

The Solution

Could it really be so easy? Could we possibly rewrite a few laws and change the world? I think so. I think where there now exist laws which create more problems than they solve, we can create new ones that greatly reduce if not eliminate the stresses from crime we currently experience. Open your mind to a new world of possibilities or to at least one basic concept which is it cannot be a crime if both participants offer consent.

MARIJUANA: We must decriminalize Marijuana completely. There can be no room left for any black market in relation to producing or distributing the drug. This means Marijuana is to be legal for both medical and social use without exception. The only regulations there should be are the ones similar to Nicotine cigarettes and Alcohol. Producers and distributors should have proper permits and consumers (notice the blatant change from "users" to "consumers") should be of legal age.

To regulate the producers there are several ways to approach it. The best idea I could come up with would be to allow anyone to produce it. Just like people are allowed to brew their own beer they should be allowed to grow their own Marijuana. Where the regulation of the drug begins is at the point of sale. Producers can consume their own product but they can only sell to authorized, licensed retailers or distributors.

Deregulating the production of Marijuana will immediately eliminate the criminal industry behind it. The cartels of Mexico will no longer have to fight over the control of the border for importing their crops. The demand for their product and the profit from it will disappear because the crop will be one produced in the United States, by legal law abiding enterprises, eliminating the need for foreign producers. This will greatly reduce the power the cartels enjoy because they will no longer have the income generated from Marijuana. No income = no industry. The street gangs distributing Marijuana will be replaced by safe and clean environments like those that currently exist in California for distribution to the consumers of Medical Marijuana. Members of the cartels will have to find another line of work. As far as the law enforcement used in the Drug War, I say we keep all of them to regulate the industry or reassign them to other crime units where they can help.

The United States will have the opportunity to generate federal and local tax revenue just like they do with alcohol and nicotine. I see the only restriction to growing would be to secure the farming area to defend against theft of the product by minors. Other than securing the production there should be no other restriction. Let the rules of competition determine the businesses to survive.

When it comes to the retailers there should be two types. The first type would be the smoke shops where people consume their Marijuana in a social setting much like alcohol in bars. The second type would be more like the package retailers of alcohol where consumers would intend to consume their product elsewhere. Isn't the solution easy enough?

HARD DRUGS: Here is a touchy subject. How can we decriminalize substances that are known to cause addiction and make them available to users/consumers knowing the potential for damage to the user? This is where we must stay focused on the greater good and not allow our own personal morality to sway our decisions.

My proposal will seem to be ridiculous and impossible to many who will read this but after many years of pondering possible solutions it is the only one that can possibly work. I propose that all hard drugs be distributed to addicted users for free.

Yes, I agree it sounds absurd. But, I see hard drug users not simply as social consumers. They may start out as social consumers but if they continue to use, eventually they are no longer choosing to use, they move to the category we consider a disease... addiction. I think we can all agree that once a person is addicted they no longer can be treated the same as a normal consumer. They must be thought of as a patient in need of treatment.

I have already discussed the criminal industry behind the production and distribution of drugs and the need to eliminate it. With addiction many times the user themselves will need to join the ranks of producer or distributor to afford their addiction. In order to avoid the user from becoming the provider the drug must be made affordable or free. In the case where a user commits other crimes those crimes cannot go unpunished. What I am talking about is the user who can get their meth or heroin from a controlled facility and will not need to create their own lab nor produce their own meth. Users will not have to commit other crimes to afford their habit.

Providing a controlled environment for distribution eliminates the public health hazards created by meth labs. Innocent neighbors will no longer be inhaling the fumes or be at risk of an explosion. The burn units of hospitals will no longer have to deal with the results from an exploded meth lab. Law enforcement will not have to clean up the hazardous waste produced.

Most of us have heard the term "crack whore" and know what it means. Females addicted to hard drugs will often turn to prostitution to afford their habit. Providing affordable or free drugs to addicted females will not bring an end to prostitution. It might greatly reduce the number of addicted females choosing prostitution simply to afford their addiction.

There is a need for a two part program in dealing with hard drugs. Maybe it is provided to social users at the normal price but in the case of a medically diagnosed addicted person they are provided for free. It is well known in every city throughout the world which neighborhoods are the areas of hard drug use. I say we zone those neighborhoods for licenses to distribute the hard drugs. I'm definitely not recommending we put heroin or meth shops next to every package liquor store. I think if the usage already exists in the area then it is already recognized as such an area by users and can continue without any inconvenience to the non-using public. Just like we regulate pornographic shops not allowing them near schools and liquor stores away from places of worship, we should regulate hard drug neighborhoods. In any event it will end the criminal enterprise behind hard drugs and eliminate most of the problems.

When creating the final policies involved with hard drugs, no policy should ever be one that will create a black market for the drug. We cannot at any point allow for the criminal industry and black market to have an opportunity to return or the entire effort will be in vain.

PROSTITUTION: When it comes to prostitution I can say it will never be eliminated. We must come to terms with it, accept that it will always exist and choose to allow it with regulations.

The success of our current policies can be seen in the mass graves found in Albuquerque, NM. Over a dozen bodies were found of young ladies of whom many were known prostitutes. Regardless of the reason they chose to become prostitutes they were people. They were someone's daughter, sister, cousin, or friend. If they were allowed to operate in a safe environment they would still be here. Prostitute or not, was it not a basic human right for physical protection?

Personally, I do not condone the choice of prostitution, just like I do not agree with the choice to use hard drugs. I do not wish for my daughters or the daughters of anyone out there to ever choose such a profession. I would also like to add that I have never chosen to take advantage of the services of a prostitute. On two different occasions in my life I have been solicited by a prostitute.

Once was when I was a young man in the Navy stationed in Great Lakes, IL. It was there that my friends and I were at a hotel just wanting to get away from base for a while and blow off some steam. We were greeted by a group of girls staying at the same motel. We originally thought they just wanted to party with some Navy guys. It soon became apparent that they were professionals. Once we realized the situation my friends and I soon made our exit.

Before we exited I did have a chance to speak with one of the girls. I made it perfectly clear that I was not interested in her services but asked if I could just talk to her for a bit. I was curious as to how she ended up as a prostitute. She proceeded to tell me she had two kids and the dad had skipped out on them. She did not have any family to help and a job at the local fast food joint would not support her and her kids. She said this is the best way she can make sure her and her kids have a place to live and food to eat.

The other instance was much more recent. It happened on a trip to Las Vegas, NV. The men in my family decided to take a cousin of mine to Las Vegas to celebrate his 21st birthday. While there we went to one of the more popular clubs. We consumed a lot of alcohol, like most people do for such a celebration, when much to my surprise I find a friend of mine from college in the club. There was a girl in their group that at first I thought was a friend of theirs. We all continued to drink and socialize when she became very friendly with me. I thought it was nothing but playful flirting with no real intention. As the night was reaching a point where many of the people in my group were making their way to a restaurant for the traditional post bar, I'm drunk and need to eat, breakfast I ended up standing alone with her for moment. I think two of my friends were in the restroom, I'll admit I had a lot to drink and the memory is a little fuzzy. But, as we stood there alone she approached me with a totally different, somewhat serious but equally nervous expression on her face. I don't remember what small talk I made with her but at a certain point she looked me directly in the eyes and said, "$1000 and we can do anything you want until you get on the plane tomorrow." I was surprised to say the least. Before I could stop myself I said something that I was later embarrassed about because it must have sounded silly to her, "Really?" She replied, "Yes...really." Then all at once I was over the shock and was able to compose myself. I responded with confidence, "I'm sure you are well worth it but I don't pay to play." She was obviously disappointed but I'm sure she had heard something similar before. I can't fathom the idea that there are too many people that will choose to use the service of a prostitute. I then proceeded to tell her that I understood that she was working and the night was still young so I would not be offended if she needed to move on to another possible client.

Since the more recent incident, I have had many questions enter my mind. It was strange that I had not really recalled the original incident until the incident in Las Vegas. I could not help but wonder just how many of the women in the night club were prostitutes? I thought it was kind of unfair to the non-professional men and women who were there. I mean what if you were a single lady there open to the possibility of meeting a man? You should not have to compete against professionals. It is also unfair for the men who waste their time with ladies, only to find out later they are professionals, when they are not interested in their services.

I ended up on a flight back with another friend and in the course of the conversation the incident came up. He laughed and explained that a couple of girls did the same thing to him and his friends. They decided that any ladies that were too friendly were professionals and he and his friends would question any women before they would continue to spend their time.

I do remember at one point in the evening, way before I knew she was working, she said she was not from Las Vegas. I had asked her how she ended up in Las Vegas and she replied, "I came out here and ran out of money."

It made me think that maybe prostitution was the result of desperate financial situations. Then I remembered an HBO special that reported on a legal prostitution business in Nevada. The girls that were interviewed in the program were not in desperate situations. They simply chose the profession based on the amount of money they could make. So obviously there is a demand for the services of a prostitute. As we know from the earlier discussions about demand for drugs, where there is a demand there will be someone willing to fill the demand.

At least the prostitutes in the legal business were required to test for STD's on a regular basis. They and their clients were also in a much safer environment. The prostitute did not have to worry about violence against her and neither would her client. In the controlled environment the use of condoms could also be monitored. So the point could be made that legalizing and regulating would provide safety for both parties involved. The one fault I found with the regulations in Nevada was the area where the prostitutes were allowed to operate was so far away from where all the potential clients were that it allowed for the continued black market operations within the city limits. Just as in the case of drugs, the regulations involving prostitutes should not allow for the continued existence of a black market for their profession. If the professionals were still allowed to operate in public arenas they should be required to identify themselves as a prostitute and also be required to meet their client at a licensed place of business. Such requirements could eliminate any potential problems and not create any inconvenience for either of the parties involved.

People around the world can eliminate much of the crime which currently exists in their communities by simply changing how they choose to address the problems of Drugs and Prostitution. Together we can make this world a safer place for all if we can open our minds to more effective laws. We must admit certain industries that we consider criminal will never be eliminated and therefore must be accommodated and regulated. We should never allow a black market to exist in these industries because the multiplying effect it has on crime. We are fully capable to make the necessary changes and it is time. Again, I would like to restate, it is not a crime if both parties consent.

Religion

When it comes to spirituality I believe it is a personal issue for each individual and should remain personal. What should it matter to anyone what I or anyone else for that matter, believes. With that said, it is religion that I have a problem with because it is religion that is a burden on our species. When you read the following you will understand why I came to despise religion and why I think it will eventually be a discarded as an unimportant piece of human history. The concepts promoted by religions are ancient and outdated. They hold no truths and they must be recognized for their inability to prove anything. Humanity is in its infancy and the fairytales offered by religion have been our comfort while we have made our way out of the caves, but if we are to continue to progress as a species we must evolve past such infantile beliefs.

I think it is also important to note, for the Americans reading this work, if you study the history you will understand that our country was not founded on Christian principles as many believe. The majority of the founding fathers were Deists, which means they believed in God but did not support religion. The Separation of Church and State, which is the very thing that protects an individual's right to practice their religion is also the very thing which protects our government from being controlled by a single religious belief. With the continued pestering of politics by the Christian Conservatives it might very well be time for the second enlightenment. It is not required to be Christian to be President, the constitution protects it.

The Problem

EMPTY PROMISE/EMPTY THREAT: For most people, religion is not really important to them until they, or someone close to them, get sick or are dying. Then in a moment of desperation they turn to their spirituality or mistakenly to their religion. I think it would be safe to assume these are the same people I saw show up only to the important holiday masses while conveniently missing the rest. I was raised Catholic and know well the types of people church goers refer to as Holiday Catholics, because we were Holiday Catholics ourselves. I always noticed that my parents would take us to Church for Easter and a few Sundays after and repeat the process for Christmas. During my research of religions I visited a Mosque and during a conversation with two devout Muslims I was informed that Islam has the same type of Holiday Muslims. I am sure the same would hold true for any religion. As each faith has the Holiday faithful they also share in having their extremists. Just like we cannot blame all Christians when the Christian extremists assassinate doctors at an abortion clinic we should not hold the entire Islamic world responsible for the terrorist acts of their extremists.

From my earliest memories I can recall looking around the Church during the mass and noticed that most of the people were not really paying attention. I figured if they were not going to pay attention then neither would I. I placed my head on the pew in front of me and stared at the floor. Amazingly, it had the opposite effect and I actually started to pay attention to what the priest was saying. I was only around eight or nine years old and even at such a young age I could not believe what I heard. At the core of the sermon was the concept of belief without question. The priest proceeded to tell the congregation, or at least those who were paying attention, that it was a sin to challenge the teachings of the church because the teachings were the word of God. As they put it, to challenge the word of God was a sin punishable by an eternity in hell. In my studies, this threat was later found to be shared in all religions in one form or another. Islam would go so far as to say it was punishable not only by an eternity in hell but in capital punishment here on earth. In other words Muslims will kill their followers if they challenge the word of God or as the Muslims refer to Him, Allah.

On the other hand, if you choose to commit to their perspective religion (I'm speaking of all religions again) and follow all of their rules you will be rewarded. No the reward is not in this life time, don't be silly, that would require a verifiable reward, and such an award would require effort and something of value on their part. No, the reward they offer is one of Heaven. Heaven as they describe it is an eternity of paradise in the afterlife. There is no pain in Heaven and all your wants are received. Islam will go so far as to promise the men who die in the name of their Holy War a reward of seventy virgins. I wonder if the females of Islam would receive the same. I guess if the women were given seventy virgin males it would not be thought of as a reward but more of a punishment for obvious reasons. Either way, I thought it was incredible that this man standing in front of all these people had the nerve to say such things. How is it that he thought the people in the church could ever possibly believe him? But as I looked around the Church I could see people buying into what he was preaching. Maybe the life they lived was not what they wanted and the lure of something better was too great to pass up? Maybe the threat of the possibility of something worse was just too much of a burden? Just follow the rationalization the believer would go through at this point. Choose to follow their rules and get rewarded or choose not to and you would be punished, not just in this lifetime but forever. Well, the same concept was drilled into us as children to "behave and I will buy you an ice cream cone or don't behave and I will spank you!"

It is at the point of the promise and the threat that the problem begins. In my studies I noticed at every point where there was an unanswered question, where they had no logical answer, the religious leaders would just make one up. I noticed many of the religious answers previously held to be true were proved false by modern science verifying they were fictitious. I also noticed that pretty much everything else in the religious works was made up. Even when the story revolved around an actual event the religion would grossly exaggerate the story to the point where it became fictional. Religion is fiction?

Realizing the amount of fiction involved with religious works I came to understand the promise of heaven and the threat of hell were not real. They were an empty promise and an empty threat.

I ask you the reader, whether you are a believer or not does not matter, to open your mind to the following idea. I do not believe that anyone who has ever existed previously on this planet or in existence now can prove heaven, hell or any type of afterlife actually exists. If no one can prove there is any type of afterlife then the spiritual leaders or prophets were simply guessing. Wow, what a revelation, the basis of all major and minor religions which exist now or in the past were all based on guesses. Think about it, does anyone really know anything more than another about an afterlife? This means the prophets of each religion had no more insight than you or I. It means none of the religious leaders who claim to know the truth are any better suited to have obtained such knowledge than the rest of us. Why should I believe anyone who makes any such claim to such knowledge if they never have to prove themselves? In no other area of human life do we allow information to be accepted without proof.

The promise of Heaven is an empty promise. Since the religious leaders have never known more than we do then any claim to such knowledge must be a blatant and outright lie. I know there will be people who desire for the afterlife and heaven to be true to the point where they are willing to accept a lie or at least not to challenge it. To those people I will offer the following: Let us say that you are a young and committed Muslim. You will see why I choose Islam for the example in a moment but please understand the example applies to all religions. Your Imam has called for a Holy War against enemies he refers to as infidels. First, it must be recognized that he has created an enemy out of people whose only threat to him are a difference in religious belief. We will visit divisions later in this work. It is widely known throughout the world of the promise, to the Holy Warriors if they lose their life in the name of the Holy War, of seventy virgins. Now, the question I would have to ask is why would the religious leader not want to sacrifice his own life in the war and receive his seventy virgins? Why is it only the followers who are asked to make such a sacrifice? If the leader is so convinced of his cause and the rewards he claims are waiting for the Holy Warriors, then why is he not willing to be the first to give his life? I often hear Christians laugh at the idea of seventy virgins while their beliefs of an afterlife are just as ridiculous. To put it simply, the Arab world is experiencing the same kind of Dark Ages which gripped Europe not too long ago. Muslims today are being sent on their version of the Christian crusades. So Christians have been just as gullible as many of the Muslims are being today. It is all a tremendous waste of human life and holds back the progress of our species.

If there is no Heaven then, there is no Hell, so do not be scared into religion by some fool preaching about such a threat, because if you listen long enough they will tell you that no matter what you do in this life their God is a forgiving God and salvation is possible for you anyway. Which means the threat of Hell is an empty threat whether you are religious or not. Beware of the propagandists who will claim," The greatest trick the Devil can play is to convince the world he does not exist." This is the greatest statement of propaganda any religion has ever created because without a Devil there could be no God, and without a God you do not need religion.

REMOVES RESPONSIBILITY: How is it we are to improve the world we live in if more than half of our species believes what comes after this life is more important than what happens here. How is it we are to get people to behave in a respectable manner when two of the largest world religions are willing to either forgive or award murder?

Are you confused? How many times have you heard the story about a murderer finding Christ and, according to his Preacher, Pastor, Priest or whatever title the person chooses to go by, is forgiven for his crimes? Islam on the other hand will award for murder in its Holy War especially if the person loses their life in the act. This particular topic could be expanded into its own book so for the sake of this work will be left to someone else to expand upon.

Forgiving or awarding murder are the extremes of religions removing responsibility for ones actions. But, it does not have to be so extreme to be detrimental to society.

It is my experience that when dealing with a religious person in business they are the ones to be regarded with the most suspicion. While I was a contractor the only lien I ever had to place on a person's home for non-payment was a Christian man who preached to me daily during the entire time I worked on his project.

He and his family asked why I was not religious. They said something bad must have happened in my life for me to lose my faith. I proceeded to tell them about my Aunt Connie. She was not a perfect person by any means, so I will not promote her like so many people will do for the deceased. She had her flaws but she also was amazing in her own right. I think a good test of just how much a person has contributed to the world is by the number of people who attend their funeral. Her funeral was beyond standing room only. Many people were forced to remain outside the church during the service and could only pay respects in a procession like line that took well over an hour to complete. It was a tremendous show of respect for a woman who never held a political office or any other position of power. She was merely a person who did the best with what she had. She was very active in the community with children's sports teams and was a team mother for many. She was very good at raising money for them. Her impact was such that even when her son was not on a team the coaches and parents of the team who knew her looked to her for help.

After explaining who she was as a person I then told them that she battled Breast Cancer for eight years before she passed. I use the word passed as if it was some calm and painless event. The truth is she suffered miserably. The cancer spread into her brain and even leaked out the top of her skull. I have to say she was one of my favorite people, I miss her dearly and I have yet to come across a person who can tell me of any crime she committed that would justify the suffering she endured. I continued to tell them her parents, my grandparents on my mother's side, have seen three of their children pass as adults. Their two sons were murdered. At the very same time my grandmother was battling cancer herself.

My aunt and my grandmother attended church regularly and were basically good people. They were neither protected nor rewarded for their faith. My aunt suffered one of the most horrible and painful deaths imaginable. What crimes had they committed to be punished so severely? (My grandmother also lost her fight with cancer, suffered miserably and died. I miss her and our conversations; she too was one of my favorite people.) I simply explained that I could not see any possible evidence of a God in my life because the innocent suffered. I told them I could never support any God who would allow such suffering to take place by people devoted to Him.

They responded with a story of their own. His wife's sister had been raped and murdered. Her body had been dumped in a ditch. Tossed out like a piece of debris. They told me it was during that trying time they found comfort in Jesus. They claimed it was Jesus that helped them through it. I could only ask where was Jesus, where was God when her sister needed them? They had no real answer for me. Any logical answer would have diminished the strength they placed in their faith. They could only say that some people are evil and innocents are sometimes victims. If I had thought there was any possible way the conversation could be a logical one, I would have asked if they thought the people who raped and tortured her sister should be forgiven if they found Jesus?

I got my answer to such a question when towards the end of the job someone stole a vehicle from them. This was a material object and not a person. It was replaceable by insurance. It was not a death. It was not a murder. It was not the absolute end to a person's life. The man responded by grabbing his gun and driving around the entire town he lived in looking for the culprits. When he could not find them, which the chances of finding them were ridiculously slim at best, he claimed it was Jesus; it was God that hid them from him to save him from doing something stupid. One thing he did say was God will punish them for their deeds, a statement in conflict with his own preaching of forgiveness.

Such contradictions in what religious people believe should be punished and what should be forgiven is exactly how religion removes responsibility. I know many of the loan officers who wrote the "No Doc" loans that created the crisis and recession were well aware of their clients inability to pay such loans. As with most criminals they justified it in one way or another and went to church on Sunday. Their preacher assured them, as they all do, that they were good people for coming to church and for giving money to the church. They were absolved of their sins by the church.

Look at the street gang members and you will find some common markings on the flesh of many of them. I constantly see tattoos of Jesus, the Cross, and the Virgin

Mary. These are the same people committing crimes of property and person. They are people to be feared. Yet the religious will absolve them of all their sins, let's not fool ourselves here they are crimes not sins, if only they accept Jesus as their Lord and Savior.

I know of a couple who were raised Catholic who changed their faith to Christian. I must recognize the ignorance in such a claim because Catholics are Christians but for some reason they believed their brand of Christianity was somehow superior to Catholicism. After becoming Christian they became estranged from their family. They would not attend most family events. When they did they were the cause of much of the friction within the family. They felt free to gossip about one family member to another. Each one of their ill intentions seemed to be justified in their mind by the fact that they were Christian and the rest of the family was not. Somehow, because they went to a certain church on Sunday they were forgiven for the trouble they caused during the week prior.

I once stayed the night at a preacher's home. During my one night stay I witnessed the preacher toss one of his children across the room for falling on his brother. As uncomfortable as I felt about the event, I tried to write it off as maybe an overreaction at the spur of the moment. The next morning the preacher's wife was serving cereal to her children. I was still lying in bed but I could hear the conversation from where I lay. The child refused to clasp his hands together for the pre-meal prayer. She promptly reached across the table and slapped him. I must say that when it comes to raising children I do believe in discipline. Children should be raised knowing there are consequences for their actions, but my point is how can these people claim to be something more than anyone else when they are no better? My problems with the preacher and his wife did not end there, the overall living conditions would have been an issue for any Health and Human services. I think they truly believed that no matter how they acted in their private life they were excused for it because he was a preacher. There were other indiscretions by the preacher for which he never has taken responsibility.

If the truly good people are not protected, and the people of questionable character or criminal action are never held responsible, then religion itself is criminal and should be held ultimately responsible.

CREATES DIVISIONS: Religions create divisions. From the obvious conflicts between the different religions to the divisions that exist within any particular religion itself. The differing in beliefs can even create political divisions in secular countries where religion by law is restricted from politics. The divisions can even reach down to within a family.

Two of the major religions are in a standoff that has been around since a man named Mohamed slept in a cave a few times and claimed to have visions of an angel who directed him to create Islam. I apologize for the over simplification but details aside that is basically what happened. No attention was paid to the fact that a person in modern times claiming such visions and choosing the odd behavior of sleeping in a cave rather than in his home with his family would be considered in need of Psychiatric attention. The "he was nuts," theory aside the divisions his beliefs created were immediate as the Muslim believers set out on a missions to conquer or kill all non believers. Personally, I never understood the idea that any God so powerful to create all that is would need the help of a simple earthly ape species known as homo-sapiens to assert His control. I also cannot understand a creator of such a magnificent thing we know as the universe, which thanks to the Hubble Telescope we now know holds billions of galaxies of billions of stars which makes our planet and our entire solar system merely insignificant flakes of dust in relation to the sheer size of the universe, would require the worship of humanity. I digress; even if we ignore the silliness of religion, the divisions of this previously new religion continue to cause wars and death. It has the entire Middle East in conflict with the largely Christian west when at the core they share the same teachings.

The Muslims conquered as far as they could during the European Dark Ages. Then in response Christian Europe sent the Crusades. This process has been repeated every so many years hidden amongst politics but still at the core a religious conflict.

There is no need for an outside, opposing religious view for divisions to exist. The divisions continue from within the religions of Christianity and Islam. Islam almost immediately broke into two opposing views upon the death of Mohamed. These two opposing views are based in a power struggle and continue to wreak havoc on the Islam world to this day. Sunni and Shiite will just as soon attack each other as they would a western infidel. Christianity faced its own upheaval with Martin Luther. Eventually Christian Europe would go to war and almost wipe out all of the young men of reproductive age. It took Europe several decades to recover. The same kind of infighting can be found in every faith. Even the peaceful Buddhist monks have gone to war with each other.

The divisions can also reach to the family level. Sometimes conversions by a family member to a different faith can create conflict within a family.

It comes down to the team concept. People become part of one "team" and root for the team without regard to the problems it creates. It you do not think the simple idea of the team concept applies to religion then you must not be aware of people who have fought, started riots or killed for the sports team of which they are a fan. If people are willing to act violently over sports then religion is no different unless it is more extreme.

It is time to choose humanity as your team and root for our overall victory.

RECRUITMENT AND RETENTION (THE PURSUIT OF POWER): Each religion seeks to validate their teachings by recruiting and retaining followers. On several occasions I can remember preachers, priests and members of the congregation of the different religious functions I attended say they must spread the word of God. Islam, as I stated before did not seek to recruit but to conquer, and force submission to Islam. Basically the recruitment and retention of members is a pursuit of power. My question would be, should we allow religions to gain in power? Christianity brought about the Dark Ages in Europe. In our modern world, Islam controlled countries suffer from human rights violations and, for the non-oil producing countries', weak economies. Anywhere religion gains control of politics the people suffer.

I believe the pursuit of power is motivated by two basic things. First, religious leaders feed their ego by the position. When a man or woman can stand in front of a congregation of thousands of people every week they must feel like a rock star. So the first motivation is based in the ego. The second is financial. I see Pastors driving luxury cars and living in luxurious mansions which have been afforded by the generosity of their followers and not from any real work. I have driven by multi-million dollar Mega Churches and Cathedrals paid for by the donations of the congregation. The so called charitable contributions are spent on recruiting and retaining members for the sake of power and wealth. Only a fraction of the funds, if any, is spent on actual charitable actions. Spending the contributions on recruitment material and Mega Churches should be criminal. In no way are people being fed, housed, clothed or cured which are true charitable actions.

Whether the religious leaders truly believe in their faith or not, the one thing they realize is their own personal power and wealth are in direct relation to the size of their following, so the motivation to spread the word will always end up one of personal gain.

DRAINS RESOURCES: Historically, all faiths have supported policies to keep their subjects in poverty or near poverty, because when there are no alternatives people turn to their faith. Supporting poverty keeps the power within the religious organization. As well, spiritual organizations usually hold a position of charity in their countries, a position not validated by their actions. The majority of monies and resources collected by the religious organizations support recruitment and retention. Salaries, publications, and opulent real estate are the outcomes of much of the donations made. I still hold a vivid memory of the Priest giving a sermon on donations to the Church. I can remember him say, "What you give to the Church will come back to you tenfold." As soon as the words left his mouth, he paused to gage the reaction from the congregation. With the lack of opposition from the faithful he stepped up the fervor in his speech. He got bolder and went as far as to say Jesus himself parted with the material of this world. Many people in the church began to reach for their wallets and checkbooks. The only effect it had on me was disgust.

It was not long ago when one of the Television Preachers in the US made headlines with an affair. During the media coverage many of the questionable practices of the modern ministries came to the attention of the press. Many modern religious leaders become wealthy by creating large followings for their organization. There were even allegations where the preachers pets lived in air conditioned dog houses. Religious leaders use their speaking ability to coerce their followers into making donations, sometimes large enough to be detrimental to the followers' ability to support them self and they do so without conscience or concern for their followers. In no way does the religious organization ever intend to return any product or service of real value to the donators or to anyone else. They will use the funds to further their true objective of accumulating more power through recruitment and retention efforts.

I have experience with the so called charity of faith based charities. I have witnessed missions who deprive their patrons of sleep and require attendance of services in order to receive meals and a place to sleep. The military uses the same type of indoctrination into military service. First they break down the individual and then they rebuild them into their ways. It is a dangerous system of indoctrination but it works. I have overheard a conversation between two "managers" of a mission for the homeless where they spoke about an individual who had "escaped" the night before. I want to emphasize the fact that the word "escaped" was used. I questioned some of the others and they were timid in their responses. They were obviously intimidated to answer if there was a possibility they could be heard by the so called managers. Through our discussion I learned of very strict rules to living at the mission. These individuals became free labor to the mission who would in turn bid jobs for painting and other handyman services. If they refused to partake in the free labor they would be booted out of the mission. The reason some of the patrons had to "escape" was because they would be met with intimidation and threats if they chose to openly leave the mission.

I would ask the readers of this work to do one simple task. Open your phone book and count the number of religious organizations in your area. I live in a small city and I counted around 500. Having been a contractor and worked all over the city I was well aware of most of the organizations through my travels. There are several structures around town worth several million dollars. I figure in a city of around 650,000 people if only half attend services weekly and only donate $1, the Church's take is $325,000 per week or $16,900,000 per year. Almost $17 million from which the majority is spent on salaries for the church leaders, recruiting new members, and building new, larger more elaborate institutions of indoctrination. Let's look at the national numbers. Approximately 300 million people in the US equal $150 million estimated donations per week, or $7.8 billion per year. I would love to see the actual numbers; I would think the number would be much larger.

Just imagine what could be done with $7.8 billion per year. Eradicate homelessness? Pay for a portion of the health insurance premiums for the uninsured if not the entire premium?

When even the smallest of congregations can accumulate tens of thousands of dollars each year, it is easy to see the ability these funds could have in the proper charitable institutions.

The Solution

SPIRITUALITY SHOULD BE FREE: I watched a program on the History Channel called God vs. Satan: The Seven Deadly Sins, where they discussed in detail the sin of Pride. Pride is considered the worst of all sins and it is believed all sins ultimately can be traced to Pride. What is it if not Pride that is at the core of Religion itself? It is the Pride of the leaders and the preachers (no matter what religion) that drives the religion. Like it was stated earlier, all religions seek new members in attempt to validate their teachings, how prideful. All things within organized religion bear a cost. The costs can be measured in time, sacrifice and monetarily. To aid religions in eliminating themselves from the very sin they preach against, they should not be allowed to impose, in any way shape or form, any cost on their followers. Religions should not collect money or require any amount of time to be devoted to the religion. They should never ask for any dedication to prayer or any other action. Leaders should never receive an income whether directly or indirectly from their position or participation in any religious activity including preaching. The income of all participants of religion should come from an actual job outside of the religion and not derive from their religious participation. The wealth of the religious institutions should be taxed. It is a disgusting waste of resources to have a structure dedicated to religious services that sits empty more days than it is put to use, and they still call themselves a charitable organization? Basically, religions should be freed from their sin of pride and forced back to their origins, spirituality, and spirituality should be free.

One World One Tribe

The purpose of this entire work was/is to create an organization within the United States and around the world committed to the continued advancement of our species. We are apes, granted we are the most advanced ape, or species for that matter, on the planet; we are still genetically defined as apes. We are tied to our planet, environment, and all other species as well as to each other. We came from caves to dominate our world and the through social and technological advancements have achieved amazing accomplishments. Our accomplishments continue to redefine the world as we know it. As I promote continued advancement and the abandonment of the many of the ancient beliefs there is one ancient social structure that I believe can be tweaked a bit and applied to our modern world. It is the concept of the Tribe.

As humans have evolved many social and political structures have been attempted. We now know that Communism and Fascism do not work. Although they did provide some short term success they ultimately could not survive. Dictatorships can provide some stability but the costs to freedom and the concentration of power lead very bad things. Royalty is merely another form of dictatorship. Republics and democracies can offer the best form of government but the very freedom they offer distorts the role of the government and the responsibilities we have as citizens. Out of all of the different types of governments I still choose democracies and republics because it offers the best opportunity for the best quality of life.

SUMMARY AND REVIEW: A necessary component to successful democracies/republics is the education of the citizens. I don't mean just the access to public education but to the education of the responsibilities of each individual within such governments. Often times the individual resigns to have the politicians deal with the responsibility which leads to many problems. Currently in the United States we are experiencing such a situation. The people elected a President with anticipation of the President solving the financial crisis. Progress has been made but has not lived up to the expectations of the citizens. The people retaliated in the midterm election by ousting many of the politicians of the party in power. The citizens leaned away from the liberals and moderates to embrace more extreme conservatives. Conservatives focused on the slow rate of recovery as a failure on the part of the party in power while never divulging any better plan than continuing the "Trickle Down," economics of the Reagan/Bush era, which has proven itself a failure. People remain ignorant to the actions and control of the wealthy by continuing to support the conservative agenda all the while complaining about the effects of such an agenda. They question, "Where are all the good paying jobs?" at the same time the wealthy class promotes shipping jobs overseas as their first move in a process that will ultimately destroy the labor in the United States. It is blatantly apparent to me that the people of the United States have forgotten the history of what the country was like before unions. Many people despise unions today and see them as a detriment to the financial health of a company while offering no other option. I offered option earlier in this work. The point is, it is left to the citizens to accept the responsibility of any and all problems. It is time to remember that in a Free Market Economy; Labor (Working Class and Middle Class) is Free to stand up for itself. If Labor stands up and says they will no longer tolerate the deportation or the threat of deportation of jobs it will not happen because Labor is the majority and still has the right to vote. When any country is left to the politicians and people of means to control, then control they will. We want a better world but we want the government to provide it while at the same time we ask they not tax us or the wealthy. We have been misled because taxes are necessary. A country cannot reach first world status without the tax base to provide the services. Imagine a United States where the following does not exist; FDA, DEA, FBI, SEC, Federal Highway, ARMY, NAVY, Air Force, Marines, etc. Manufacturing jobs are a necessary component to the strength of any country and should never be allowed to leave and taxes should be paid. The wealthier a person is the more they have used the resources provided by taxes and therefore should pay a greater amount. The current economic policies in the United States as a whole will eventually break labor once and for all and create a third world country of peasants and lords. But, this can be avoided if we so choose.

At the same time the War on Drugs and policies against prostitution has been the Crusade of the politicians. They create hard line policies and claim they are fighting the good fight, while the policies actually create more problems than they solve. Consent needs to be the determining factor in deciding whether an action is a crime or not. You would not consent to be murdered, robbed, abused, or raped. Those are actions where there is no possible way a person would agree to or offer consent. On the other hand a person could consent to offering money for the services of a prostitute or accepting money to provide the service. A person could consent to pay for a product, Marijuana for example and since there is consent from the buyer the action of providing the product should not be a crime. Should these industries be regulated? Of course they should be regulated but they should not be criminalized any more than Alcohol.

Religion has hidden behind the guise of charity while spending their wealth on recruitment and retention and should no longer be allowed to operate in such a manner. Taxes should be imposed on the wealth of religious institutions and leaders should not be allowed to accept any sort of income. Spirituality should be free and there should be a "Don't pay to pray," policy adopted by everyone.

Knowing such things summarized here, we must take action to halt destructive tendencies and policies. We must act to first save the beacon of freedom know as the United States then continue the policies throughout the world to create a more cohesive global society. Some countries have progressed in certain areas beyond the United States and I for one am embarrassed by it.

We humans are capable of tremendous greatness. Our strength is only limited by our unity. It is time we unify with one common goal, the advancement of our species. In order to do so we must define the world in which we wish to live.

ONE WORLD ONE TRIBE: One World One Tribe shall be organized as a non-partisan charitable organization. Inspired by the structure of the tribe it will support policies which allow for personal ambitions but do not allow such ambitions to come at the expense of other members of the tribe. Since we all originate out of Africa, and it is believed from the same tribe, we will consider all the people of the world part of the tribe without regard to political boundaries, ethnic or racial groups. Religions shall play no part and sexuality will be irrelevant.

The Mission

Economic:

1. Organize a not for profit health insurance company.
2. End for profit correctional facilities.
3. Encourage/assist labor to organize.
   a. Demand profit sharing
   b. Demand 50% representation on board of directors.
4. Assist in the creation of cooperatives.
5. Require all trade partners to have the same minimum wage/benefits as the highest minimum wage/benefits of participating countries.

Crime:

1. End the drug war by legalizing all drugs and choosing regulation over criminalization.
2. Legalize and regulate prostitution.
3. Never create laws which promote the creation of a criminal industry.

Religion:

1. Tax all income and assets of religious organizations which are used to recruit or retain members.

2. No taxes on funds used for verifiable charitable acts.

The Tribal Pledge:

As a member of the Tribe I pledge to accept the responsibility for the continued progress of our species and agree to adhere to the following principles:

I will:

1. Support companies who profit share whenever possible.
2. Demand profit sharing from my employer and equal representation for labor.
3. Choose to partake in a cooperative for employment if at all possible.
4. Choose to destroy the criminal organizations by removing their profit from illegal drugs and prostitution.
5. Never donate to a religious organization because spirituality should be free. Instead my donations will go to my local school system.
6. Be free to keep my belief in a Creator if I so choose while rejecting religious teachings and scriptures.
7. Use my own morality and compassion as my guide.
8. Reject any practice or policy which interferes with the progress of the human species.

This is not the end but the beginning.

Join

The Revolution

@

OWOTrevolution.org